2020 WORDS OF PANDEMIC POETRY

2020 WORDS OF PANDEMIC POETRY

DALLAS ANN H. ERWOOD

LitPrime Solutions
21250 Hawthorne Blvd
Suite 500, Torrance, CA 90503
www.litprime.com
Phone: 1-800-981-9893

© 2021 Dallas Ann H. Erwood. All rights reserved.

No part of this book may be reproduced, stored in a retrieval system, or transmitted by any means without the written permission of the author.

Published by LitPrime Solutions   09/01/2021

ISBN: 978-1-955944-09-0(sc)
ISBN: 978-1-955944-10-6(e)

Library of Congress Control Number: 2021918061

Any people depicted in stock imagery provided by iStock are models, and such images are being used for illustrative purposes only.

Certain stock imagery © iStock.

Because of the dynamic nature of the Internet, any web addresses or links contained in this book may have changed since publication and may no longer be valid. The views expressed in this work are solely those of the author and do not necessarily reflect the views of the publisher, and the publisher hereby disclaims any responsibility for them.

CONTENTS

Forward ix
Pandemic Mornings 1
Goddesses of Peace, Nieces I Love to Pieces 3
Today's 86'Ing 5
Ruth Bader Ginsberg 7
Don't Panic in a Pandemic 9
Pandemic Poem (Too Much News) 11
Their Last Date 13
Poetic Pleas 15
Things I've Learned 17
Almost Cut My Hair 19
All In God's Time 21
I'm Sorry 23
Sprinkles Of Mom 25
News Junky Blues 27
Happy Mother's Day 29
The Palm Desert Post Office 31
Kissed 33
Joker 35

Zeitgeist 37

Wonderful Wishes 39

Titleless 41

Defund Da Fuzz 43

Ariana & Demitri 45

August 47

Unicorns & Lollipops 49

In 2020 51

My Covid Couch 53

Thanksgiving '20 55

Mistletoe (To Jennie) 57

Dedication: To Rick,
For sticking with me through thick and thin
And for literally being the wick to my flame

FORWARD

During the pandemic of 2020, I took a few writing labs, a journaling course, and then I decided to participate in NaNoWriMo, which is the National Novel Writers Month; every November, writers commit to writing 50,000 words during the 30 days of November, which works out to 1,666 words a day, and that's one short story a day, for me. It being my first NaNoWriMo attempt, I did pretty well on that pace until my husband ended up in the hospital with pneumonia, but not Covid! So I stopped with the novel writing, and went to the poetry I'd been writing— more like word doodles— during the pandemic, and serendipitously, my poems contained exactly 2020 words!

PANDEMIC MORNINGS

This social distancing
Is a real pain in the brain,
A real ache in the neck,
And a real sore spot in my lower back!

When I prayed for "Peace in 2020"
On my Christmas cards in 2019,
I did not visualize
This in my mind

But i've never experienced such peace
As these pandemic mornings
Sunrise walking
& a complete lack of traffic

I wrote a book last year
My dad's WWII story
I want to make one thing clear:
Dad gets all the glory

GODDESSES OF PEACE, NIECES I LOVE TO PIECES

Goddess mom
Of double delights
Jazzy & strong
Huffy & tall
Holly go lightly
All the day long

Goddess mommy
Hillary the lovely,
All brown & big
A beautiful olive
Mediterranean West
She's simply the best

Goddess wife
Loves her life
Cooks & curates
Works & plays
Perfect mates
In all ways

Always, Auntie Dallie

TODAY'S 86'ING

I got 86'd today
Outta the Coffee Bean & Tea Leaf
For a tickle in my throat,
So I turned to cough in my elbow.

What an honor!
The pretty barista,
With big, brown eyes
Round as a doe's, goes:

"Can you please use
The mobile app outside
Cuz of your cough?"
"OK," I go.

So I turn to exit
At her request.
Keep healthy, my friends,
While the whole world mends.

RUTH BADER GINSBERG

May I recommend
On The Basis Of Sex
In this climate
Of sheltering in place

The clothes
The cars
The kids
The arguments

The ending!
The twists
The turns
The law

The word "freedom"
Isn't in the Constitution!!
Radical Social Change
Ruth's the truth!!!

DON'T PANIC IN A PANDEMIC

My little Linus pendants
He's holding his security blanket
Two I hung on some hoops.
So I put on my rain boots

Off to the grocer I go
Face mask around my throat
In the gray pouring-down rain
Of another pandemic day

I notice one of my earrings gone!
I try real hard not to panic!!
I'm as methodical as James Bond
In the middle of a pandemic

I search one whole grocery store
I file a missing-earring report
I go to the second store
And I find it on the floor!!!

PANDEMIC POEM (TOO MUCH NEWS)

What a predicament!
A worldwide pandemic!!
It feels like being caught
Naked and on top!!!

Will Katie Porter please
Pass out all the pennies
Straight to the employees
And bypass the brass?

Shaking hands is for sissies
Ya bunch a cold fishies
Simply hug your own shoulders
And then bump elbows

We've been brought to our knees
Not a bad place to be
A little humble pie
Here's to spit in your eye!

THEIR LAST DATE

On October 30,
2019
Julia Ann Erwood,
Had a date with her king

At 10:00 p.m.
She met him in heaven
She was not late
For that date with her mate

He was a WWII Sub Vet
She, a goddess of the domestic
They had 3 boy descendants
2 judges & an architect

They danced the golden streets
After her final sweet surrender
Their love was so neat,
So true & so tender.

POETIC PLEAS

My favorite memory
Of my dad and me
Was the time
He told me the story

Of my namesake,
His nurse in WWII,
Dallas Fellersen,
Who nursed him to health again

He was shot
Through the shoulder
At the Anzio invasion
In the European theatre

He was 21,
She was 10 years older
And he was very,
Very fond of her

THINGS I'VE LEARNED

The things I've learned
During this 2020 pandemic
Almost make me
An epidemic academic!

There's Venmo, the currency current
And Apple Pay via Wallet
There's Zelle & there's Zoom
So we can stay put and halt it!

But honestly, I prefer
To be safe at home with my hubby
Maintaining our distance & washing hands
Until I get too crabby

But best of all is Instagram
And my mobile CBTL app
Like my mom with the microwave
It takes me a while to adapt!

ALMOST CUT MY HAIR

I dyed my hair today
Became the Breck girl again!
But who I really wannabe
Is a flapper from the Roaring Twenties

She was so gucci-gucci
A supermodel ahead of her time
I'm so fascinated with that era
When my parents became alive!

Edna St. Vincent Millay
William Somerset Maugham
Ernest Hemingway
Nancy Hanks Hufstader, my mom

And thanks to James C. Hinkle
I can do whatever I want
Except go visit my family
So I'm going to cut my hair!

ALL IN GOD'S TIME

This is for all
My sisters and brothers.
It started last fall
With the death of our Mother.

It started late September,
Rick got pneumonia, then the flu,
And ended for us in December
W/a pneumonia relapse a' deux.

So today is now Easter,
A beautiful spring day.
We're all basically sequestered
The new abnormal way

Here's my prognosis
For all humankind:
It's coming up roses!
All in God's time.

I'M SORRY

I'm sorry
But I love social distancing!
No more space invasions!!
No more pernicious positioning!!!

Another beautiful day
Another bandana mask!
Another ride in the rays!!
And some more jumping jacks!!!

You are wanted, needed and loved
Understood, beautiful and beloved.
Above the angels are serving
A dinner you are so deserving!

Singing a lovely song
Comprehended by all
Into every life long
Amazing Grace will surely fall

DONE!   DALLAS

SPRINKLES OF MOM

I don't know about you
But I'm halfway through
We are six weeks in
We can do six weeks again

Twelve times seven
Equals nearly ninety days
And that's what it takes
For a human to change her ways

I'm staying home
For my niece who's having a baby
Her baby shower got postponed
I'm quarantining until her delivery

Then it's the Newsome normal
So called after California's governor
When people respect each other
And Mother Earth is my new lover

NEWS JUNKY BLUES

The presidency's poisoned
Agent Orange is in office
Pandemic poems
Epidemic mornings

Guns, diseases
Atomic bombs
Trump Pence
Drs. Drew & Oz

Surf City
Stupidity
Complete with their
Airhead mayor

I can read or write
In the middle of the night
I'm a woman on a mission
With her 2020 vision

HAPPY MOTHER'S DAY

My mom
Is the bomb
Beautiful and strong
Her spirit lives on

In my eyes
In my nose
In my choice
Of colorful clothes

In my nieces
And my sisters
Who took hold
Of her baton

Queen Mothers
To-be or gone
Keep calm
And carry on

THE PALM DESERT POST OFFICE

"I refuse to live that way,"
He said,
As I opened the door
For him,

Wearing a mask
And one glove
"So you don't
Have to touch it;

"I do it
For those who don't."
For those who won't
I will.

"What a weird way to live,"
He said
"Good for you,"
I said. Fool.

KISSED

December 7, 1941,
USA drawn in
To WWII

The Anzio invasion
May 23, 1944,
My dad got shot
Through the shoulder

D-Day
June 6, 1944,
Normandy Beach Landing

V-E Day May 8, 1945,
Victory in the European theatre
Germany surrenders

V-J Day, August 14, 1945,
Final victory in the Pacific theatre
Japan surrendered
George kisses Greta

August 14, 1948
My mom & dad
Got married & kissed

Drawing by Eileen Gianguzi
graphite & colored pencil on smooth Bristol paper

JOKER

If you are
A Batman fan
Then Joker
Is wild, man

The murder
Is madcap
The acting
Is badass

The buildup
Perfection
With his
Dancing predilection

The sets are so gothic
His laughter so caustic
His makeup so toxic
& his suit was just so sick!

ZEITGEIST

Courthouse kitties
Thelma & Louise
Thelma is special needs
Louise is special feeds

Thelma is thin
And favors him
Louise is voluptuous
And loves Dallas

Thelma is affectionate
But you can't pick her up
Louise likes a heavy pat
Like she's Jabba the Hutt

I adore their whiskers
And their iridescent eyes
The sweet, silent sisters
With their pawing, purring sighs.

WONDERFUL WISHES

Nine-nine, 55, H.A.O.
Congratulations Hillary & Joe
Weight, length & initials
Sending you wonderful wishes!

This is the name
Of the blue & white bouquet:
"Wonderful Wishes"
& Y'all can't touch this!

Ho! Your boy
Is our joy!!
Oh! My heart
Just hit restart!!!

You, like a star,
Love from afar
Shine thru the night
A bright strong light!

TITLELESS

Happy Father's Day Johnny Rose
Moira's my sartorial mentor
David's my maid of honor
And every girl's A Little Bit Alexis
Watch it on Amazon, Apple or Netflix
But not till Fall streams the final season 6!
The whole shebang is Simply The Best
For a funny fix or comedic kicks
I've had enough of all the dicks
& Janes of politics
Getting in their licks
Giving me pricks
They're all a bunch of hicks
Mixing up our mix
One of my top summer picks:
Floating down the River Styx
With all of my Rix
Unaffected by poetics
Feelings aren't facts
Says whose guru?
I could go on; but I get too blue

DEFUND DA FUZZ

Defund the police?
Pa-lease!
Trump democracy
Whirled peas

I'm a bad rapper
A midday napper
A baby boomer
A meeting zoomer

A kaleidoscope of stripper poles
The colors of a giraffe
Brown background with beige molls
The neighborhood would laugh

But I loved it! The nudist camp!!
The his and hers convertibles
The slumber parties, the Hinkle stamp:
A love that's incontrovertible!!!

ARIANA & DEMITRI

You looked like a goddess
In your wedding dress
And he your prince
Of happiness

06/27/2020

AUGUST

Time for ice cream
& babies' birthdays
A midsummer's dream
& a fire's haze.

In Covid time
It's tough to rhyme
But poetry
Is gold for me.

I miss our place
& wish I were flying
To the velvet embrace
Of The Big Island

Kona Coffee
Big blue waves
A string bikini
Rainy days

UNICORNS & LOLLIPOPS

Lollipops and unicorns 🦄🦄
Candy and books 🍬📖
Angel wings & devil horns 😈
Blessed with nice looks 😈

Thanks mom
For your beautiful smiles
Thanks dad
For your loving eyes

The Who, the zoo
The backyard bars
The concerts, culture,
Home life stars

Dillydally lallygag
Yin to my yang, zig to my zag
When you have to get a flu shot
Even unicorns get a lollipop

IN 2020

How much weight
Did you gain?

The wash your hands one,
Wear a mask to

Stay alive five,
Shelter in place eight,

Stay at home ten,
Quarantine fifteen,

Covid nineteen
2020 twenty,

The dirty hair thirty
The Fox and Friends forty

Or the fat ass 45?

MY COVID COUCH

My covid couch,
She's no slouch
She's golden, feels like velvet
Wish i could get over it!

My covid divan
From Ethan Allen
Almost a year old
I hava sore throat!

Oh, no!
Do I have a cold?
Don't want to be sick
With that damn covid!

So i sit
And I pick
At my fingertips
And watch Netflix

THANKSGIVING '20

I was thinking thankful thoughts
Rainfall just like diamond drops
A fire in our fireplace
Sunlight shining on my face

Winds of spirit, winds of air
Blowing through my heart and hair
Memories of family fun
Golfing in the Santee sun

You are wanted, needed, loved,
Understood, respected, beloved.
Angels all around us serving
Thanksgiving dinner so deserving

Snow capped mountains up up up
Cats Thelma, Lou & Sari pup,
Even with this physical distance,
Wishing you all a Merry Christmas!

MISTLETOE (TO JENNIE)

My sister and I grew up in Santee
Surrounded by flora & fauna;
The mistletoe magnetized me,
She was drawn to the pomegranate tree.

Come time for my holiday harvest,
I'd grab a few random golf clubs,
Go across the street to the riverbed golf course,
Hurl them up in the trees to release the sticky shrub.

She would hand pick the hard fruit,
Cut them in half, squeeze & stamp them on canvas
Their abstract stains inspiring her absolute,
She would paint over them, releasing her prowess.

For 25 cents a bag
Door to door I would go
Selling my red-ribbon-wrapped
Preciously mined mistletoe.

COVER ART:
"Bleeding Heart"
Pomegranate panels by Jennie Hinkle
Oil on canvas over pomegranate stain

THE END

www.ingramcontent.com/pod-product-compliance
Lightning Source LLC
Chambersburg PA
CBHW021431070526
44577CB00001B/160